JEWELL CHRISTY

Poetic Gems

ISBN: Softcover   978-1-7960-1398-6
        EBook   978-1-7960-1397-9

Print information available on the last page

Rev. date: 02/08/2019

To order additional copies of this book, contact:
Xlibris
1-888-795-4274
www.Xlibris.com
Orders@Xlibris.com

Poetic Gems

Jewell Christy

This book of Poetry, POETIC GEMS, is dedicated to my gem of a family, the Thompsons and the Owens and all that I have adopted.

TABLE OF CONTENTS

FOREWORD

Poetry is a way to make music with words from the heart. It is composed of feelings, observations, creativity, a little inspiration, and sometimes humor.

Whether it be rhyme or prose, everyone can be poetic.

WISHES

HOPES

DREAMS

JEWELS

BRIDGES

Wouldn't it be wonderful to have BRIDGES built to cross the street,
Connecting good thoughts, feelings and helpfulness?,
Bridges built across the land of honesty and safety,
Bridges built across the sea connecting continents
As in times past
Making our world a continuous connecting land of humanity.

If Bridges of understanding,communication and respect
Were built with people connections ladled with tolerance and sympathy,
And knee deep In empathy,
Then that would make sincere feelings and caring a two-way street
built with Bridges connecting everyone to everyone,
expressing hope and real Love.
This would make Bridges easier for everyone to cross.

MUSIC TICKLING MY SENSES

Delicious, healthy, scrumptious food,
Wallowing over my tongue, trying to distort my face,
Ah, this is music to my taste.
Tiny cute, damp babes in arms,
Mom's best perfume sprayed on me; oh, but I'll never tell,
Because that's sweet music to my smell.
Hearty laughs of children playing in mud.
Tall mountains green, beneath billowy clouds and blue hued skies,
Making everything just right,
Accenting my love, bringing sweet music to my sight.
Holding favorite hands, kissing little foreheads,
Brushing shoulders with those that I love so much,
This indeed is music to my touch.
Bach, Duke, B.B. King, ol' Hip Hop,
You've done well! Hurray you're all winners,
Soothing hearers forever over the years,
Even me! For that's sweetened music to my ears.

I KNOW THERE'S A STORY I JUST CAN'T PUT IT INTO WORDS

The ripples created by a rock in even the smallest stream,
Or the burning fog producing warm white steam,
I know there's a story,
I just can't put it into words.

After the rain there is the pyramid height of a new ant bed,
And the sky is a rainbowed luscious ribbon of colors appearing overhead.
I know there's a story,
I just can't put it into words.

How in blue heavens huge cotton balls float.
Though still beautiful, the blue turns gray, signaling a rain chance is remote.
I know there's a story,
I just can't put it into words.

People's plights of poverty, struggles and abuse
Conjures up the notion that sometimes living seems of no good use.
I know there's a story,
I just can't put it into words.

...I KNOW THERE'S A STORY I JUST CAN'T PUT IT INTO WORDS

Tales of terrorism and turmoil reigning uncontrollably,
Where peace is sought or at least talked about universally,
I know there's a story,
I just can't put it into words.

Where once upon a time
Finally really ends, they all lived happily ever after,
And happiness comes with tons of hearty laughter;
I know there is a story
That somebody can put into words.

A story to tell is in my heart.
Somehow it always seems to slip away,
I know, in my soul, it's written there,
I just can't say.

GUARD YOUR MIND

Guard your mind, then set it free and leave it there.
Set your mind for success and a positive attitude.
Set it for high expectations
Nix on the obstacles. Just allow your mind to exude.

Set it to excel with enthusiastic goodness,
That you may loudly to the world exclaim
The set it for peace, joy and fame that calls your name.

Set your mind, guarded, for grand possibilities for maintenance of good health,
Set it, guarded, for steady faith, then fix your focus and your stare.
Do set your mind, guarded, for happiness and victory
And then just keep it there!

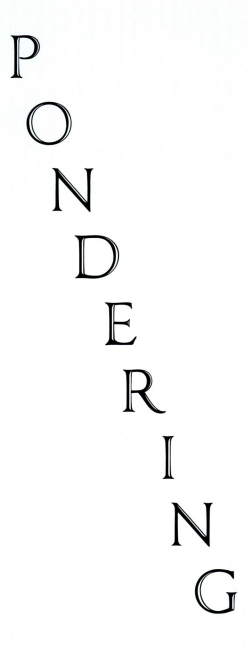

PEARLS

LOVING

I WAS lOVED WHEN I WAS A BABY.
I WAS lOVED WHEN I WAS A lADY
NOW I lOVE AS A WOMAN!

FROM THE VILLAGE

Inspire us to instill in, teach our children good things.
These are times to LOVE Them,
And be Excellent Examples - in all ways
To Keep our progenies Strong.
Help to Encourage them to Lead!!
With a worthy, caring baton to the next generation,
With Honor and Dignity,
Simply Assertively, but Gently,
PASS IT ON

LET'S DO LUNCH

When you're hungry and you want company,
And it's time to be full, happy, and worry free,
Then Let's Do Lunch!
When you've paid all of your bills and your tax,
It's your BIRTHDAY, And now it's time to really relax,
Hey, Let's Do Lunch!
We may be too late for the before noon brunch,
But don't you worry,
We'll Just Do Lunch!
You feel like chomping on something with
A delicious crunch,
Do not tarry, Let's Go Do Lunch!
How does one "do lunch or make groceries?"
These call for action but we do them with ease,
English verbs are used carefully and with
Meaning; that's my hunch,
But enough of that,
Let's eat, uh --- I mean
Let's Do Lunch!!!

I AM YOUTH
BY
JEWELL T. CHRISTY

I don't want to do anything!

I am young.

My folks say I am cute.

And that's all good, I suppose,

But don't ask me to do nothing!

I did well in school,

And now I am in college.

I studied and learned, listened to my parents and teachers

Socialized and made many good friends.

I guess I had to do Something, even if I didn't want to.

Well, now I am finished with all that,

And I just want to do absolutely NOTHING,

So, Don't even Ask.

However, in this Global Society

Hmm, I guess I Can be a good example for the younger ones.

That's not asking too much.

I can help my parents more and my grands and the older people around me.

BUT, Don't ask for Anything after that!

...I AM YOUTH

Maybe, just maybe, I can learn as much as I can as I get older,
So that I can pass that knowledge on to others,
Demonstrating through my actions, my words and my deeds,
How to be a healthy, thoughtful, serving person.
Maybe I Can be a BLESSING to others,
Therefore be a Blessing to myself.
But don't ask me to do ANYTHING Else,
Because, I just Won't DO It!
(Sigh) I Just Don't Want to Do Nothing!!!

I Am YOUTH

By J.T. Christy

Ending action:
Character pulls a phone from pajama pocket.
Character: Hello,Oh Hey! What's up? No, I'm not doing nothing.
What are you doing?

PROPS: Pajamas, Cell phone

THE ABC'S FOR YOUNG PEOPLE (OLD ONES TOO)

When we first started school, we were told we must learn the 3 R's, Reading 'Riting and, 'Rithmetic. However, we soon learned that there are other alphabets in the English Language that we must learn also.

Abstain from all evil.

Be the Best you can Be.

Care about others.

Do what's right.

Empathize with others.

Forgive and try to forget.

Give as much as you can.

Help others.

Internalize intelligence.

Jesus is the man to keep in your life.

Keep your Faith.

Let your little light shine.

Move to Enlightenment.

Never give up!

Opt to stay focused.

PRAISE THE LORD!!!

Quietly state your truths and opinions.

ABC'S FOR YOUTH

Read, Write, and Compute.

Serve.

Train your mind to Think before acting.

Understand self in order to understand others.

Vigorously search for truths.

Weed out the negative to incorporate the positive.

X-ray your thoughts and words before eXpressing them.

You are special; believe in you.

ZOOM into life with a happy spirit.

SITTING IN THE OLD CHURCH PEW

I sit in the old church pew on Sunday morning,
Listening to words of wisdom,
To guide me through the week,
Accompanied by musical utterances to abide in me,
And last for all of eternity.

Sitting in the pew, I listen intently to the pulpit words,
while peering over the fancy hats
and those in deep biblical thought
absorbed in provoked pastoral verbage.

I ponder, I meditate, I am enthralled.
I listen, I internalize it all;
On blessed Sunday mornings, this is what I do.
quietly and reverently sit in my favorite church pew.

A MIND DEFERRED

To see the handsomeness of his face
The pleasant demeanor and carefully displayed manners of good taste.
It seems so absurd that herein lies a mind deferred.
The person can't sometimes tell you his/her name and
May even have difficulty expressing their pain.
We must help them bathe and tie up their shoe,
Remind them to eat their food, or comfort them when they know not why they feel so 'blue'.
Tell them at times to join in, but we must also remember to include,
To pay attention, give inspiration, encourage them
In whatever they aspire to do.
Be patient, give assurance; don't pity, don't slight,
Empathize, avoid thinking "disturbed", for they too are God's Children,
Simply with a mind deferred.
We're the "norm", so we are to help, not hinder
We should help them blend in as much as possible,
Its time we learned to mix to gain more insight,
This not only helps them but helps us to understand their plight.
So we halt the core impatience, and selfishness
That leaves us quite disturbed,
For that certainly causes one to wonder, whose mind is really deferred?

by
Jewell Christy
2015

A RUN INTO THE WILDERNESS

To be enraged by family shouting, calling names, doing put downs,
While experiencing the somber quietness of others,
Heart-broken, disturbed with statue-like frowns.
This makes me just want to go.

To see children disobey, disrespect, be selfish to those around,
Makes me know that as parents and mentors
We are duty bound
To be examples, not blame others, but make our decisions sound.
Without this, I just want to go running.

To see injustice and biasness and know that they still exist!,
OH! Take them away now; I INSIST!
Even worse when We practice them,
And we don't see the harm, Oh Darn!
I just want to go running, screaming.

When we work in all phases to do good, give help to all the rest
Yet evil lurks to destroy and reek havoc on our given best
I just want to go running, screaming far into the wilderness.

...A RUN INTO THE WILDERNESS

What can we do before retiring

Into a horrible competitive duel?

Perhaps it would be better to simply live by the Golden Rule.

GRATITUDE

DIAMOND

BEING GRATEFUL

Just because at this moment you have the ability to think, reason, comprehend and compute,

And you've had the privilege to be presented to the world "with all faculties" to make your outstanding debut.

Just because right now, you can move, kneel, dance, enjoy yourself simply having fun,

And You can count your money, bathe yourself, walk, talk, and even run

You can be safe, eat to satisfy your hunger and tastes, and o your own go happily outside to play

Don't get so sure you'll always have these special gifts, for the Lord gives – and the Lord can take away.

Just STOP; help those who may not be as lucky as you,

And be continuously Thankful to God, no matter what yu do.

Be forever Grateful, always caring and compassionate to the "different" and disabled. Do – just give it a try,

For there only by the Grace of God, Go You and I!!

by
Jewell Christy
2015

MY MAIN MAN

He's always there, Lending an ear.
No matter what I say, He Listens and hears.
He's my main man, my confidant tried and true
Turning things happy, when its evident that I am so blue.
He's my main man.
He's constantly there to guide me through.
Whether for making ends meet,
Or for just getting me back on my feet.
On Him I have come to depend,
For this Man is truly my friend,
Whether to shower me with a little love
Or to share His nourishing food,
He makes my life feel really good.
Every hour, each minute, all of my days,
He's the Guy to whom I give All of the Praise!
HE is my SHEPHERD, who I converse with, my pal to whom I pen,
My guardian angel where my prayers I constantly send.
I'll always be HIS number one Fan,
And that makes Him- now and forever- my Main Man!

I MATURE AND SMILE

I Turned into an aged, wiser woman quick,
Not like when my youth presented me with my hair long,
And my waist not quite so thick.
Now, my hips hurt, my bones seem to have grown cold,
Alas, I realize this day,
That I am indeed growing old.
It's so difficult to walk,
I sometimes slur or repeat when I talk.
Hey, even my sexy is gone,
I just want to lie down and
Simply stay home.
With no energy, my social life is all but destroyed,
Fun times, hanging out, shopping and dancing is now null and void. I enjoyed my
youth and look forward to many more happy years, I have become a senior,
My nagging inclination is to joyfully shout, Cheers!

SENSITIVITIES

I feel the Noise,
I hear the View,
I See the Music,
And I Taste the Rumors Too.
I feel the Gladness, I Hear the Light,
I Smell the Movements, I see The Silence,
And Taste the Action with all my Might,

When All's Well that Begins Well,
That makes me Feel, See, Hear, Smell, and Simply Taste the LOVE

NATURE'S

BEAUTY

PEARLS

PASTEL RAINBOW

Half circle vivid colors touching both ends of the rugged horizon,
In hues fading into one another like issues of life blending from rough to smooth,
Sometimes two to three at a time lifting frowns to smiles- and back again.
Pastel Rainbow, not quite clear, but knowing that maybe the storm is gone for awhile,
Makes us tread waters, life waters we don't want to swim in,
life Waters- creating stress, sadness, illnesses, anxieties, fears, abuse, heartbreak,
Yet, interrupted with intermitted periods of laughter, fulfillment, peace, love, joy.
Grasp a Beaming, Multicolored Pastel Rainbow!
It's a time to enjoy.

ECHOES IN THE P. M.

This Night is enclosed in a quiet hush
Of giant sheets of darkness,
With only a speck of light peering from a moon full,
Only surrounded by flickering stars
Layered with wide drops of pouring rain
Appearing as fireflies blinking on and off.

RAINBOW CLOUDS

Rainbow Clouds present a heavenly and earthly view,
Seeming to mean God is lovingly smiling,
As HE peers at you and- me too.

Rainbows may occur after vicious storms,
Or even light gentle rains,
Showing us HIS powers and goodness,
Are only our GOD'S aims.

THE Rainbow Clouds,looking like magnificent
Strands of color with calcified, puffy cotton balls fed
Reminds us that we are promised
Of better days ahead.

BIRDS IN THE BACKYARD

The birds in the backyard,
Chirp and sing and play all day,
Through the verdant plains pecking at juicy marcels,
In the thick grass they make their way.
Power- walking on sidewalk patios,
And like fierce predators crouching at their prey.
Sitting on the backs of lawn chairs,
And leaving evidence that they have been there.
They lean on the brim of the water fountain bowl,
Slurping,gurgling and rolling back their heads,
Sternly watching slinky worms and the insects in the tall ant beds.
I am mesmerized as they follow the leader,
Flying back and forth on the communication high wires,
Even more so, as they take off in arrowhead unison
To the beautiful blue skies.
They pepper my backyard with boundless energy.
I just want them to stay,
But as I walk out to gain a closer gaze,
These lovely backyard birds simply fly away.

Printed in the United States
By Bookmasters